C000076891

GREATEST
Manc
One-
Liners

GREATEST
Manc
One-
Liners

Ian Black

BLACK & WHITE PUBLISHING

First published 2013
by Black & White Publishing Ltd
29 Ocean Drive, Edinburgh EH6 6JL

1 3 5 7 9 10 8 6 4 2   13 14 15 16

ISBN   978 1 84502 701 8

A CIP catalogue record for this book is available
from the British Library.

Typeset by RefineCatch Limited, Bungay
Printed and bound in Poland
www.hussarbooks.pl

Introduction

If you are woman (or man) enough to look a detractor, or lesser-spotted mard-arse, in the eye and say, 'I'd call you a fanny, pal, but you seem to me to lack warmth and depth,' then this may well be the very book for you.

Contained herein is a distillation of the finest of one of the skills for which Manchestahh is rightly and fondly renowned – the pointed and deliberate jibe or crackback. We are good at it. Who but a Manc would ask, 'Are you into casual sex, or should I dress up?', and where else would you be queried as to which window you wish to take your departure through? Mancs are masters of the faintly ominous, as in, 'The last thing I want to do is hurt you, scrote-face, but it's still on the list,' as well as the direct, 'You've got a face like an 'orse in the 'uff.'

Use these words if you wish, but be very, very careful on whom you use them.

Manc Questions

You have the right to remain silent, but you don't have the ability, do you?

You said 'no' to drugs, did you? They wern't listenin, were they?

Sure, I'd like to help you out,
which way did you come in?

Are you into casual sex,
or should I dress up?

And which dwarf are you?

10,000,000 sperm and you were the fastest?

With enough force, pigs fly
just grand. Want to join them?

Do you still love nature, son, despite what it did to you?

Do you want folk to accept you as you are or do you want them to like you?

I'm busy just now. Can I ignore you some other time?

What's your problem, mate?
I'm betting it's hard to
pronounce.

What am I?
Flypaper for freaks?

Nobody likes you,
surely you remember?

Manc Threats
and Insults

The last thing I want to do is hurt you. But it's still on the list.

Aye, dwarfie. You know what?
When it rains, you'll be the last
one to know.

Listen, sick'ed, when you were born they slung the kid and kept the afterbirth.

I thought I saw your name on a loaf today, but when I looked closer it said 'thick **cut**'.

Cocker, you've got a face like
an 'orse in the 'uff.

That chin of yours looks like a docker's kneecap.

When they were giving out
bellies you jumped the queue
because you thought they said
jellies, didn't you, fatso.

Your feet are so big that if you threw a shoe in the canal it would be a hazard to boats.

With those ears you look like a taxi with the doors open.

Cheer up, son, you've a face
like a wet Bank Holiday Friday.

Your bird's so ugly, she'd frighten a sailor off a raft.

If you were a McDonalds snack you would be a Filet o Fish . . . Nobody likes you, but you're always there.

WHAT THE HELL IS
THAT ON YOUR NECK?!
Ri', it's just yer head.

Whatever kind of look you
were going for, you missed.

Don't look at me that way or
I'll split you in three 'ole 'alfs.

Your teeth are like the Ten Commandments: all broken.

Instant dipstick.
Just add alcohol.

Tesco needs you.
They've run out of stupid.

I'd call you a fanny, pal, but you seem to lack warmth and depth.

Here's a pound, dipstick, go out and buy yourself a life.

Pick a window, pal,
you're leaving.

If I agreed with you
we'd both be wrong.

I didn't say it was your fault,
I said I was blaming you.

He thinks Johnny Cash is
what it costs for condoms.

Your teeth are like a row of bombed houses – since 1944.

Go away and iron your face.

God must love stupid people. He made you and millions more.

I'd like to see things from your point of view but I can't seem to get my head that far up my arse.

I don't have an attitude problem. You've got a perception problem.

You, cock, are a waste of two billion years of evolution.

If you're looking for sympathy, cocker, you'll find it in the dictionary between 'shit' an 'syphilis'.

If I wanted to hear from an
arsehole I would have farted.

Everybody has the right to be stupid, but you are abusing the privilege.

You are multi-talented.
You can talk and piss me
off at the same time.

You've got more issues
than the *Manchester
Evening News*.

Hey you, yeh, you,
the oxygen thief.

Don't annoy me. I'm running out of places to put bodies.

When they put teeth in
your mouth, they spoiled
a perfectly good arse.

Just because you've got
a prick doesn't mean you
have to act like one.

Don't play stupid with me –
I'm better at it.

You are a spherical arsehole.
No matter which way you
turn, you're an arsehole
from every angle.

With a face like yours,
every day is Halloween.

I'd like to leave you with one thought, but I'm not sure you've got anywhere to put it.

Listen, pal, I could eat a bowl of alphabet soup and shite a better argument than that.

You're just not yourself today.
I noticed the improvement.

Be yourself?
Bad advice for you, son.

I don't know what makes you
so stupid, but it's working.

If what you don't know can't hurt you, then you, yogurt, must be bloody invulnerable.

If your brain was chocolate
it wouldn't fill a Smartie.

Save your breath, you'll need it to blow up your girlfriend later on.

You've got so many slates
missing you are due a
Council grant.

You've got a mouth on yer
like a camel eating toast.

You would be out yer depth
in a car park puddle.

If you were any stupider,
we'd have to water you
twice a week.

If shite was music,
you'd be an orchestra.

Calm yerself down, boy, or Tony here will show ye the 'knife in the barmpot' trick.

I'd bet money that when you stayed at Michael Jackson's as a kid, he made you sleep in yer own bed.

Manc Names

They call him Compass –
his nose goes North an
his ears go South.

The Baker over there? The kids and the wife are gone. Now it's only him and his tart.

The Balloon is always saying:
'Don't let me down'.

He always makes a bolt for the door when it's his round – that's why they call him Blacksmith.

The Depth Charge, he's
always after a sub.

They call him The Ghost –
always moaning.

Harpic? He's clean
round the bend.

The Lame Kangaroo? He 'asn't had a jump in years.

Whenever Jigsaw is
asked to do something
he goes to pieces.

They call 'er The Olympic
Torch – she never goes out.

Deep down, she's shallow

Manc Philosophy

Don't walk behind me, for I may not lead. Don't walk ahead of me, for I may not follow. Don't walk beside me, either. Just bugger off, pal, would yer?

One big voddy, two big voddy,
three big voddy, more.
Four big voddy, five big voddy,
six big voddy, floor.

Shame about him. He's marching to the beat of a different kettle of fish.

Don't take life so seriously, lad. It isn't permanent – especially if it's yours.

I feel as if I've got a face like
a dollop of mortal sins.

Just say no. *Then* negotiate.

What's for yer won't go bye
yer, and yer deserve it,
barmpot face.

If you don't care where you are, then you're not lost.

In Miles Platting, it's sad how whole families are torn apart by simple things, like a pack of wild dogs.

I've got plenty of talent and
vision and stuff like that.
I just don't give a shit.

I'd crawl a million miles across broken glass to kiss the exhaust of the van that took her dirty knickers to the laundry.

I've got the wisdom of youth,
and the energy of old age.

Look, we all have somethin' to bring to this discussion. But I think from now on the thing you should bring is silence.

Manc Insults
to Men

He's not stupid – it's kind of like he's possessed by a retarded ghost.

He's the kind of a guy that you could use as a blueprint to build an idiot.

If he was my dog, I'd shave his arse and teach him to walk backwards.

Those scars? A lifetime of playing chicken with hatchets.

He's got a face like a forty-shilling piss pot – pure white, but all chipped.

The only big thing about 'im is 'is ears – he looks like an elephant with the wind behind him.

His ma couldn't breastfeed
him – he was curdling
the milk.

Him, he's suffering
from bottle fatigue.

Fat? He can sing a
duet on his own.

That twillop! A whore once told him she had a headache.

My Peter and sex?
This morning I used
him to time an egg.

'im, he's got an IQ of two.
It takes three to grunt.

I keep thinking, if he talks enough, someday he'll say something intelligent. Am I holding my breath? No.

My man is no good at sex,
but he's thinking of taking
it up as an 'obby.

I thought about him all day today. I was at the zoo.

I've had a really good time,
but this wasn't it, barmpot.

My Peter is good-looking,
the trouble is his teeth are
brighter than he is.

I'll never forget the first time I met him. Christ knows I keep trying.

He's so narrow-minded that
when he walks his earrings
knock together.

My Tommy? He's got
hundreds of well-wishers.
Everybody wants to throw
him down one.

Sorry, pal, I can't put small objects in my mouth or I'll choke.

Him? The only place he's ever invited to is outside.

A shag? How about never?

I'll try being nicer if you
try being better looking.

My Mick? Ye could use his prick to stitch tapestry if it wasn't attached.

He makes The Elephant Man
look like Mr Universe.

'E couldn't hit sand if
he fell off a camel.

Manc Insults
to Women

When she undresses,
you hear the Lycra
breathe a sigh of relief.

She's so ugly she tried to take a bath and the water jumped out.

She's cured hundreds
of Peeping Toms.

She's handled more balls
than Peter Schmeichel.

She's been cocked
more times than
Elmer Fudd's shotgun.

She's seen more
stiffs than Quincy.

She's so ugly she'd frighten a monkey out of a banana tree.

She's got a face that could
make an onion cry.

She's got a face that would
drive rats from a barn.

She's got more chins than a
Chinese phone book.

She's seen more Jap's eyes
than an Oriental optician.

It's like shagging the sleeve of a wizard's cloak.

She's so bandy, she couldn't stop a pig in a ginnel.

When she sucks a lemon,
the lemon pulls a face.

She's got an arse like
a bag of washing.

She wears enough
make-up to sink a ship.

She sweats like a dog in a Chinese restaurant.

She's got a face like
a stuntman's knee.

It's like shagging
a pail of water.

She's seen more cock
ends than weekends.

She's so ugly not even a sniper would take 'er out.

She's done more lengths
than Duncan Goodhew.

Even the tide wouldn't
take 'er out.

She's got more fingerprints on
'er than Scotland Yard.

She's had more seamen than
Liverpool docks.

She couldn't find water
if she fell out of a boat.

The finest woman who ever
walked the streets.